Table of Contents

Disclaimer

Incipient Thoughts

The organization culture represents an enchanting composite of norms, values, rules, and expectations that control the way in which individuals and teams work toward the same goals, shared qualities, and response to distinct actions.

The relationship between culture and leadership is defined by team members' performance and effectiveness.

The philosophy and the mission of an organization are key factors in defining the organization culture.

If the organization is to be faithful to its philosophy and mission, its leader's style must be consistent with them.

An important key to successful leadership is to know how, when, and how much of what leadership style is needed in a particular situation.

An autocratic leadership style in a democratic organization can create chaos.

This is why we should know to choose the appropriate leadership styles for each situation.

There are so many different types of leadership styles that dominate this world and bring a unique sort of value.

We have seen so many types of leaders in our history.

They all conquered their world using the power of empathy and communication.

Think about the representative image of Germany of 20th century, where hundreds of thousands of Germans were wildly cheering their Fuhrer in Leni Reifenstahl's brilliant and terrifying 1939 Nazi propaganda film, "Triumph of the Will".

Think about Franklin Roosevelt's impact on a nation paralyzed by economic depression. He admitted that "We have nothing to fear but fear itself", combatting the skepticism of his followers.

They were notable representations of magnificent motivational leaders working their magic through their speeches.

They had the inner motivation to change their world because that was their purpose.

The leader's purpose is to change mentalities and make others understand the positive impact of change.

Their leadership style needs to reflect the mission, goals, values, and philosophy of the organization.

Discovering your skills or the lack of proficiency in some areas, the leader determines the most effective way of leading his team.

Chapter 1: How Good Are Your Leadership Skills?

"If your actions inspire others to dream more, learn more, do more and become more, you are a leader"

-John Quincy Adams

What's your key area for improvement?

Who do you consider to be a great leader?

Maybe it's a famous businessperson, a religious figure, a war hero, or even a politician.

Or maybe you have a model in your personal life like your father/teacher or a close friend. You can find people leading almost everywhere you look.

However, having the responsibilities of a leader and dealing with them doesn't necessarily transform a person into an effective leader.

Hard work, determination, and the practice of emotional intelligence can determine whether people lead effectively.

Leaders can improve their leadership skills and performance in specific areas by identifying where they are already professionals and exploring the unshaped skills that need further development.

How Good Are Your Leadership Skills?

"While a good leader sustains momentum, a great leader increases it."-John C. Maxwell

I have prepared a technique that will help leaders discover their level of performance and areas that need enhancement.

Here, you have 18 statements.

1. When you assign tasks, do you consider people's skills and interests?

2. Do you doubt yourself and the ability to succeed?

3. Do you expect nothing less than top-notch results from people?

4. Do you expect people to work harder than you do?

5. When someone is upset, do you try to understand his/her feelings?

6. When circumstances change, do you struggle to find new ways to deal with changes?

7. You think that personal feelings should not be allowed to get in the way of performance and productivity.

8. You are highly motivated because you have all it takes to be successful.

9. Time spent worrying about team morale is time that's wasted.

10. You get upset and often worried in the workplace.

11. Your actions show people what you want from them.

12.When working with a team, you encourage everyone to work toward the same overall objectives.

13.You set expectations for your rules – it's easier than being the enforcer all the time!

14.You enjoy planning for the future

15.You feel threatened when someone criticizes you.

16.You make time to learn what people need from you so they can become successful.

17.You're optimistic about life so you can see beyond temporary setbacks and problems.

18.You think that teams perform best when individuals keep doing the same tasks and perfecting them, instead of learning new skills and challenging them.

Giving sincere answers to these statements, you will find what skills you should develop as a leaders, what kind of competencies you should use, and which leadership style fits your personality type and the type of authority you have now within an organization.

In this way, you can adjust your behavior and your abilities to lead according to the leadership style you choose to exercise.

Personal Characteristics

There are many leadership skills and competences that transform you into an effective leader. You can develop each of these skills within you.

Triumphant leaders tend to have certain traits that make them different from others.

There are two keys areas of personal growth and development that create the foundation of a successful leading process: *self-confidence* and *positive attitude*.

People who are self-confident are very inspiring and like to surround themselves with individuals who believe in their power of changing things.

If you are a positive and confident person, you will find it much easier to motivate people to do their best.

Self-confidence

(Questions 2, 8)

If you are disappointed by the answers to these questions, it means that you have to work on your self-confidence because it is built by conquering meaningful skills, facing hard situations, and knowing how to add value to the work you do.

Improving your self-confidence means to become more aware of all your strengths and skills that you have already acquired through challenging experiences.

Positive Attitude and Outlook

(Questions 10, 17)

It is said that positive mindset is related to strong leadership.

Being positive means more than having a happy face all the time in front of people. It means to develop a powerful sense of balance and identify the setbacks and problems and accept that they occur with the aim of making a difference in your attitude, and make you strong.

Positive people embrace every situation realistically and they are ready to make the necessary changes to prevail over problems, whereas negative people become stressed and see the situation as more complicated than it is. Negative attitudes lead to fear, worry, distress, and inevitability to failure.

In this situation, you need to understand your thinking patterns and work on the faulty parts of your personality, identifying and eliminating the negative thinking.

Thought Awareness, Rational Thinking, and Positive Thinking

Our perception about a situation can influence the way perceive it, feel about it, and react toward it. Our perception might be right or wrong.

Sometimes, we may be unreasonably harsh with ourselves or may jump to wrong conclusions about people's motives. This can cause problems and destroy our confidence, leading to unhappiness or unfair behaviors with others.

Richards Lazarus came up with a simple definition of stress, which is highly valuable today. *"Stress occurs when someone thinks that the demands on him exceed the personal and social resources that the individual is able to mobilize"*

When it comes to stress, people make two conclusive judgments:

1. *They feel very threatened by the situation they have to overcome*

2. *They must judge whether their capabilities and resources are sufficient to meet the threat.*

The level of stress someone feels depends on how much impair he thinks the situation can cause to him and.

Perception is the key impetus that distorts the impact of the situation on the stress level. The interpretation determines the level of stress someone will feel toward a difficult situation.

Stress and emotions are parts of the early warning system that puts us on guard about the threat of these situations.

Thought Awareness

The negative thinking develops from our fear of failure when we put ourselves down, criticize our errors, and doubt our abilities, excepting failure as an obvious outcome.

In our tormented mind, the negative thinking damages our confidence, harms our performance, and paralyzes our mental skills.

A significant problem of negative thoughts is that they filter our consciousness, causing damage and flitting back out again, creating a harmful impact that will be crystal clear over time.

Thought awareness is one of the most effective processes of observing and analyzing the stream of thoughts in stressful situations.

You should practice it in a moment when you feel you're ravaged by negative thoughts that distort your rationality.

When the moment comes, let your thoughts run their course while observing them and their impact, writing any aspect you have noticed about them in the following worksheet as they occur:

Negative Thoughts	Rational Thoughts	Positive Thoughts

Another useful tool that will help you become more aware of your negative thoughts and their impact is the Stress Diary, where you keep track of your thoughts in unpleasant moments and then analyze their intrusion. Logging your thoughts for a long period of time helps you determine well-marked patterns in negative thoughts and at the end of the period, you will be able to establish judgment toward the common thoughts that can cause damage. Tackle them as a priority and try to manage them as much as you can.

Rational Thinking

The next step in dealing with negative thoughts is to challenge every thought you wrote on the worksheet and ask yourself if that thought is reasonable or not.

Analyzing your Stress Diary, you may distinguish the following negative thoughts:

1.The feeling of dissimilarity/ contradiction

2 . Worries that your job performance is not good enough

3. Anxiety that the things outside your control can diminish your efforts

4 . Worries about other people's reactions to your work

And now I will help you overcome your fears and negative thoughts:

1. Feeling of contradiction:

Have you trained and educated yourself for the job position you have right now?

Do you have the necessary resources and experience you need to do it effectively? I think you know now.

And if you know that you have done everything you could do, why are you still worried?

Are you setting unreasonable standards regarding your job?

2. Worries about job performance

Do you have the training required to do a good job?

Have you planned it appropriately?

Do you have the knowledge and resources you need to succeed in your job?

Have you established the time you need?

If you haven't, then you should do it quickly. If you did it, then you're performing at high standards, but you weren't aware of it.

3. Problems with issues outside your control

Have you managed contingency planning appropriately?

Did you confront the risks and contingencies suitably? If so, you are prepared to solve any potential problem.

4. Worries about other people's reactions

If you are well prepared to do your job and you do this efficiently, there's nothing else you can do.

If you are fair with people and you know that you are focused on your responsibilities within the organization, this is something outside your control.

Positive Thinking and Opportunity Seeking

The final step for defying negative thinking is to use the rational, positive thoughts and affirmations. It will help you see the bright side of any situation and reach opportunities instead of failures.

Affirmations are the motive of building self-confidence. Using them, you can erase the damage of negative thinking.

Positive Affirmations:

1. Feeling of contradiction/inadequacy: "I know that I'm very well trained and I have the experience, tools, and resources I need. I can do a really good job."

2. Worries about performance: "I am well informed about the problem and I can understand it. I have the time, resources, and knowledge to deal with it. I will do an amazing job."

3. Problems with issues outside your control: "We have considered everything that could happen and we have planned how we can deal with contingencies. Everyone is ready to help. We can react flexibly and effectively to unforeseen events."

4. Worry about people's reactions: "I am well prepared and I am doing the best I can. I know that fair people will treat it with respect. At any unfair criticism, I will respond with professionalism and maturity."

This process will help you overcome fears and negativism and pin down any opportunity where there is no light to uncover it.

Focusing on positive thoughts will help you bring positive events and people into your life and it will increase work performance.

Emotional Intelligence

(Questions 5, 15)

This concept is more than a skill, it is a specific kind of human talent.

It is the ability to recognize your and someone else's feelings and use them to create strong relationships.

One of the most important ingredients is empathy.

This will help you achieve a clear understanding of someone else's perspective. If you are not satisfied with your answers, I will help you work on your level of emotional intelligence.

Providing a Compelling Vision of the Future

(Questions 6, 14)

It is the ability to shape a robust and compelling vision of the future and lead people through it. The first step of implementing an inspiring vision is to gain knowledge in the area you're operating on. To create a vision, you have to learn how to lead people from the front, building the expert power.

Building Expert Power — Lead from the Front

"Power isn't control at all--power is strength, and giving that strength to others. A leader isn't someone who forces others to make him stronger; a leader is someone willing to give his strength to others that they may have the strength to stand on their own." -Beth Revis

A good use of strategic analysis techniques can help you gain the key comprehension of the needs in the environment you are working in and into the need of clients.

There are many powerful bases a leader can use, such as the power to give reward, punish, control information, and the power of position.

These types of power have the strength to put the person leaded in an unhealthy position of weakness while leaders can feel autocratic.

Thinking about the evolution of society over the last 50 years, you can notice that employees are more powerful and they don't like to be leaders in a way that can affect their personality and values and they will do what they can to undermine people who use these sorts of power.

But there are also three types of positive power that effective leader can use: charismatic power, expert power, and referent power.

The most important power in the leadership mission is the expert power because people will always look at a leader for direction and guidance.

They trust their leader and his ability to lead in a constructive direction, giving substantial/strong advice and getting fruitful results.

If the members of the team perceive the leader as an expert, they will listen to him when he is trying to inspire and persuade.

If they consider the leader an expert, they will be motivated to respect his expertise when he shows them how to work productively. They will respect his judgment when helping them to achieve tremendous results from their work, and they will believe in the wisdom and knowledge when he coaches them motivation and performance.

How to Build Expert Power

The first pitch in building expert power is gaining expertise.

You will achieve it by gathering information. There is nothing more powerful than information. Effective information gathering is the basic perspective-widening tool an efficient leader requires.

Gaining good quality information transforms a manager into a great leader.

Leaders operate with innovative ideas, so accomplishing them, he will create an information pattern from which marvelous ideas emerge.

1. Promoting an image of expertise, the leader will make sure that his team, peers, and superiors are aware of his/ her formal education, significant work experience, and achievements.

An efficacious way to achieve it is to display diplomas, licenses, and awards as a mark of expertise in the office.

They emphasize the struggle to achieve results and gain knowledge. You will get credit for it.

Another idea is to adapt a sagacious tactic in which you refer to your experience and educations: "When I was a CEO in that organization, we had a similar problem".

2. Once you have gained credibility, you should maintain it because your image of expertise depends on it.

Acting confidently and decisively in a crisis is the print of an efficient leader who knows how to cope with a problem. If you can't deal with a problem, people will lose the trust in you and your influence.

3. Keep informed

Expert power is reflected in our rational persuasion and demonstration of expertise. Rational persuasion is based on your ability to respond smartly to problems.

4. Recognize team members' concerns.

5. Avoid threatening the self-esteem of subordinates.

In the process of arguing for their valuable ideas, some leaders can behave as they are smart and only their ideas count for the development of the organization, while team members are just ignorant people who have to accept and respect leaders' decisions.

Try to avoid this type of behavior. People chose you for your ability to inspire, envision, enlist, embody, empower, evaluate, and encourage.

Motivating People to Deliver the Vision

(Questions 9, 12)

This is linked to creating and selling a vision. You have to conquer techniques of convincing other to accept the objectives you have set. Sharpen teamwork and accept that when people work together, they can achieve greater results.

There are two big tools you can use to provide effective leadership by correlating performance with team work: Management by Objectives (MBO) and Key Performance Indicators (KPIs).

Being a Good Role Model

(Questions 4, 11)

"The quality of a leader is reflected in the standards they set for themselves".- Ray Kroc

Good leaders lead by example. They are very transparent in their attitude and they make sure their words correspond to their actions. They assume the consequences of what they say. People follow them because they see that the leaders' outcomes came from an enlivening vision combined with hard work, integrity, and morality.

They are constantly involved the organization's tasks and they stay in touch with what's happening throughout it.

A great leader is not the one who sits in the chair in his office and gives orders, but the one who demonstrates the values and actions he expects from his team. He makes the expectations he has clear and shows them the path/direction to get there.

As with building vision, a primary part of being a good role model is leading from the front by developing expert power.

His authority is not given by the position he manages in the organization, but by his ability to enforce his authority and power through concrete value.

Managing Performance Effectively

(Questions 3, 13)

"High expectations are the key to everything".-Sam Walton

Effective leaders manage performance by setting their performance standards clearly.

High performance is achieved when everyone knows the responsibilities and the desired outcome.

You can also create rules and help the team understand why you have chosen those rules.

Involve people in the process of rule-making because they will feel that their words really count when it comes to making decisions.

You should also help them understand the expectations by comparing them with the resources assigned for the task.

Apply the rules you have set fairly and consistently.

Providing Support and Stimulation

(Questions 1, 7, 16, 18)

Motivating teams is more than giving them a list of tasks that has to be completed every day. They need to be challenged and motivated to work.

They need to learn new techniques, develop new skills, gain more knowledge, and feel supported in their efforts to do an extraordinary job.

Think about the way you allocate tasks and look for opportunities to match people with jobs and responsibilities that will ensure their development and growth.

There is a formidable tool that will help you decide when and how to support team members and make them shine.

Remember, also, that the emotional support plays a fundamental role in the teamwork.

One of the most useful tools for finding the balance between concern for people and concern for work productivity is the Blake-Mouton Managerial Grid. And we will discuss it in the next chapters.

Chapter 2: Leadership Motivation Tools

"Leaders must be close enough to relate to others, but far enough ahead to motivate them."

-John C. Maxwell

In life, it doesn't matter where you're coming from but where you manage to get.

Where are you going and how are you going to get there?

Aside from what you want to accomplish, what kind of person do you want to be as a result of your actions and efforts?

These are the questions you have to ask yourself before taking a path.

People who achieve marvelous things in life are unfailingly those who give a lot of thought to their own evolution and growth.

They become extraordinary people by design, not by accident.

They are like diamonds. The raw material is polished and shaped continually, until it becomes shiny and indestructible.

In the same way, they continually shape and polish their character/personality until they evolve and grow into someone important and worthwhile.

And so should you!

The highest goal you can share is to become a great leader, a magnificent person who is looked up to, admired, and respected by others.

If you want to become more of a leader but you're finding it difficult or, more than this, impossible to motivate yourself, it is the right time to start challenging it.

Motivational leadership is more than an attitude, it is a strategy to uplift and inspire people to achieve high performance. Personal leadership, on the other hand, is the power to motivate yourself to do things that can improve the quality of your life. Both of them are required to achieve maximum performance. They are the opposite sides of the same coin.

The starting point of personal leadership is to start seeing yourself as a role model, as an example for your team.

Start seeing yourself as the person who sets the standards for others.

A key leadership characteristic is to set high standards of accountability for yourself and lead by example, as you are always around, secretly taking notes about the way they act and react.

Motivational leadership is built on the law of indirect effort. It is easier to achieve things in life by indirect means than by direct means.

You can become a leader for others more easily by demonstrating that you have the knowledge and the qualities the leadership position requires than by ordering others to follow your directions.

The first step in building the motivation to lead is to find out what demotivates you and then find a solution for the problem.

Find out what holds you back. Look within yourself for answers. What if you find that you are not sure that you want to lead a team even if the benefits of leadership are enormous?

Maybe you feel uncomfortable in your role and you are confused about the expectations you have to meet.

Demotivation arises also from the day-to-day irritations that distract you from doing a good job.

You may feel that you cannot improve your work, bring bright ideas, and are distracted every time you want to focus on your work.

Maybe you have lost your motivation. Analyze yourself. Try to understand the factors that influence this problem. Then work on them.

I will give you a useful tool that will help you determine the level of motivation you have for leading people.

Demotivation Demolisher

You just need 15 minutes to note down the things that steal your motivation; these are things that erase the motivation to lead or general irritants that are undermining the self-motivation.

De-Motivator	Circumstantial or Habitual	Solution
Fill in with demotivators	Choose from those causes, which one is circumstantial and which one is habitual	Find solutions and write them here!

Now that you finished the list, you have to take on the challenge of tackling the killjoys.

Start by listing each of the demotivators as circumstantial and habitual. The circumstantial things are determined by circumstantial factors such the disease of someone you love. Habitual things are more common and they spring from the working style such as unfinished tasks or too many responsibilities.

Then go to the solution column. If there are circumstantial factors that bother you, then you should identify them and neutralize their impact. If there is a recurrent habit, try to understand it and correct/change it.

The Need-Effort Bridge-Link Action to Motive

The best way to create motivation is to establish a clear vision for the actions you take. In the moment when you will realize that your efforts fulfill the need you have, the effort will automatically turn into a valuable reason.

If you realize you cannot do anything more about the majority of your demotivators, then it is time to discover why you are continuing to accept these demotivators. It may be because you have set a very strong, meaningful need for your effort.

There is a quick need-effort establishment exercise you can do every time you feel that you need it: take a piece of paper, divide it into two halves, and on the top of the first part, write "Needs" and on the other half, write "Effort".

Take a few minutes to complete the list with needs like material rewards, professional standards, or personal targets and the list with efforts like those you are making on your job, in your community, or others.

Then link the efforts with the needs they serve. Remember that the more significant the need you are seeking to satisfy, the more motivated you will feel.

Once you have finished the exercise, you will find a strong motivation to justify your efforts. You may have to spend energy combating the killjoys, but you know that the effort is worth it.

Passion Propulsion-Find your passion

Use it to inspire and enthuse

Passion is one of the most powerful motivators. Being fiercely passionate about the goals and targets helps give you an edge, but passion can be destructive if it is not handled with precision.

You should discover your passions and then use them as a laser sharp focus to achieve your goals.

The next step is to identify the goals you are passionate about and find out how to direct your passion energy in accomplishing them.

1. Define your passions

Find out what fires you up. If you find it difficult to give a right and definite answer, take 30 minutes to answer to these questions:

a) What would I want my life to be like when I am 60?

b) What do I want to have accomplished 5 years from now?

c) What are the three things I would want to do if I only had 6 months to live?

Try to answer to these questions, because you will find your fierce goals, the ones you should naturally be passionate about achieving.

If not, you may need to set goals that are on a higher scale.

2. Harness passion energy

Once you have set specific goals, try to find out what you need to do to achieve them.

Determine the key information and training you need to accomplish them effectively.

List the tools you will need in the process and the people you will need support from as you work on your goals.

Create a professional, rational, well-thought plan to turn your goals into reality.

Chapter 3: Core Leadership Theories

Learning the foundations of leadership

Maybe you're wondering why some leaders are successful while others fail.

There is no magic combination of characteristics that makes a leader successful. Different characteristics matter in different circumstances.

1. The four core theory groups

Trait theories claim that effective leaders share a number of common personality attributes or traits.

The old traits theories argued that leadership is an innate quality that you do or don't have, but the new approaches tend to focus on the process of learning about how we can develop leadership qualities within ourselves and others.

Trait theories help us define or identify traits and qualities such as integrity, empathy, assertiveness, likeability, and right decision-making skills that will shape the profile of a successful leader.

However, none of these traits, nor any specific mixture of them, will ensure success as a leader.

Traits are external behaviors that arise within our minds and it's these internal beliefs and processes that are important for effective leadership.

2. Behavioral theories — What does a good leader do?

Behavioral theories analyze leaders' behaviors.

In the 1930's, Kurl Lewin developed a framework based on leaders' behavior.

He argued that there are three types of leaders:

1. *Autocratic* leaders make decisions without consulting their teams. This leadership style is considered appropriate when decisions need to be made quickly, when there is no need for input from others, and the team agreement is unnecessary in achieving a great outcome.
2. *Democratic* leaders ask for input from their team before making decisions, although the degree of input can vary from leader to leader. This leadership style is used when the leader considers the team's perspectives essential in his decisions, but it can be difficult to manage where there are lots of different perspectives and ideas.
3. *Laissez-faire* leaders don't participate at the process of taking decisions. They allow trustworthy people to make many of the decisions. This works very well only when the team is highly capable, motivated and doesn't need

close supervision. This style of leadership can fail because most of these leaders are lazy or distracted.

The way leaders behave affects team performance, and, in turn, the company's performance.

The most effective leaders are those who can use many different behavioral styles and choose the right style for each situation. They adapt their behaviors.

3. Contingency Theories — How can the situation influence good leadership?

None of the leadership types are comprehensive; the best leadership style depends on the situation.

The theories I have been talking about try to predict which style is productive and valuable in a given situation.

When you need to make rakish decisions, which style is perfect?

When you need full support of your team, which is the most effective way to lead?

When talking about the leadership style, how should leaders be more people-oriented or task-oriented?

Contingency theories discuss these questions and provide valuable answers.

There is an effective tool called Hersey-Blanchard Situational Leadership Theory that links the leadership style with the maturity of individual members of the leader's team

4. Power and influence theories — What is the source of the leader's power?

There are two different leadership theories that reflect the way leaders use their power and influence to get things done.

French and Raven's five forms of power reflect the three types of position power*: legitimate, reward, and coercitive*; and two sources of personal power: *expert and referent* (personal appeal or charm).

This is the best well-known power theory with a strong impact on the leadership styles.

This model highlights the impact of using personal power for developing the expert power.

Transactional leadership is another strong leadership style that uses power and influence, assuming people do things for reward and other reasons. It is also focused on creating tasks and reward structures. This style works, even if is not the most appealing leadership strategy in terms of creating strong bonds, relationships, and developing highly effective/motivated teams.

Most of the leaders today use this technique of reward on a daily basis to get things done.

Chapter 4: Effective Leadership Styles

Choosing the right approach for the situation

There are so many ways of leading people, each one with its specific characteristics.

But businesspeople have developed strong frameworks that reflect the main leadership styles.

By understanding these frameworks, you can develop your own leadership approach and become an effective leader as a result.

1. The Blake-Mouton Managerial Grid

The Blake-Mouton Managerial Grid was published in 1964 and it is the most important guide for choosing the leadership style, based on the concern for your people and efficiency in production or tasks.

Some leaders are very task-oriented, they simply want to get things done, and some leaders are people-oriented, they want people to be happy/satisfied with their work.

Some leaders combine the previous leadership styles. I think that this is the luckiest and the most effective leadership approach.

If you like leading by setting and implementing tight schedules, you tend to be more production-oriented or task-oriented. If your priority is people and trying to fit to their needs, then you are more people-oriented.

There is no wrong preference, just as no leadership style is best for all situations.

However, it is very useful to understand which leadership style fits in your situation, so you can start working on improving your skills.

There is a very efficient framework that analyzes the tendencies leaders have when it comes to task versus people orientation.

It highlights the degree of task-focus versus person-focus and identifies five combinations of different leadership styles.

The Managerial Grid

It is based on two behavioral dimensions:

1. *Concern for people*, where the leaders considers the needs of team members, their interests, and distinct areas of personal development when taking decisions for a specific task.
2. *Concern for results*, where the leader considers the concrete objectives, organizational performance, and efficiency when

deciding the best solution for accomplishing a task.

There are two axes for creating the Managerial Grid:

- First one highlights the leadership concerns for results
- The second one focuses on people, defining five leadership styles:

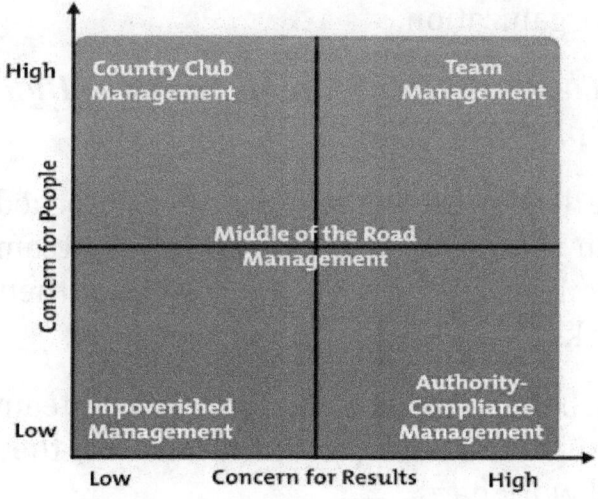

*. Impoverished Management — Low Results/Low People

This leadership style is the most ineffective one.

The leader doesn't master the ability of creating systems for getting the job done, nor for creating a work environment that can satisfy or motivate people to work effectively.

The outcome is disharmony and disorganization.

*. Country Club Management — High People/Low Results

The leader of this category is concerned with the needs and interests of his team members and less on the results of their work.

His beliefs are that as long as the team members are happy and motivated, they will work hard.

In reality, the productivity suffers a lot as a result of the very relaxed environment and also from the lack of direction and control.

*. Authority-Compliance Management — High Results/Low People

These leaders believe that people are only a means to an end.

The efficiency and productivity at the workplace is more important than employees' needs and satisfaction.

This leadership type is very autocratic and has strict rules and procedures. The form of motivating people is through punishments.

*. Middle-of-the-road Management — Medium Results/Medium People

It seems that this combination between the two competing concerns is an ideal compromise.

But this is the problem: When you compromise, you give away a bit of each concern. In this way, you don't fully meet the needs of people and the performance of the production.

The leaders who adopt this style are focused on achieving average performance and often believe that this is the most efficient one.

### *.	Team Leadership	—	High Production/High People

According to the Blake-Mouton model, this is the best managerial model.

These leaders focus their attention on production needs and the needs of the people in an equal and high manner.

The aim of this approach is to make people understand the organization's objectives and become involved in establishing the organization purposes.

When employees are committed and contribute to the organization's success, their need and production needs coincide.

This type of environment is the most effective one because it is based on trust, support, and mutual respect, and leads to high motivation and satisfaction, and as a result, high outcomes.

2. How to apply the Blake-Mouton Managerial Grid

It is important to know and understand the various approaches of leadership, so you can improve the way you perform as a manager in the company.

Understanding your current situation helps you identify the less effective areas of your leadership style.

Step 1. Determine your leadership style

Think of some recent situations when you acted like a leader.

For each one, place yourself on the grid according to where you believe you fit.

Step 2. Identify areas of improvement and develop your leadership skills

Analyze your current leadership approach and think about the impact it has in the context.

Try to find ways to improve it. Are you setting for the "middle-of-the-road" because you think this is the easiest way?

Find ways to get the skills you need to reach the position of Team Leadership.

This means to be focused on problem solving, involving others, too, or improving your communication skills if you think you are too task-oriented.

Maybe you have to enhance the way you schedule or monitor projects progress, if you think you are too people-oriented.

Monitor your efficiency continually and watch for situations when you turn back to your old habits.

Step 3. Put the Grid in context

It is essential to know that the Team Management style is not always so efficient and it needs to be completed by democratic or participative leadership to fulfill employee and company's expectations.

If a company is the midst of a merger or another crucial change, the best approach is the one that is focused more on people than on production.

Likewise, when the company has to face an economic crux, employee needs may be placed on the back burner, for the short-term at least, to accomplish good results and enhanced productivity.

This framework is very practical and efficient.

It highlights the differences between "concern on results" leadership and "concern on people" leadership and establishes five leadership styles.

The model proposes that when both people and outcome concerns are high, productivity of the company and employee engagement increase at the same rate.

In my opinion, this framework is the starting point to an inner debate about your productivity and performance as a leader. It tells you clearly which leadership skills you should improve for fitting in the best leadership style: the Team Leadership style that combines high productivity with highly motivated and engaged people.

Chapter 5: The Hersey-Blanchard Situational Leadership Theory

Choosing the right leadership style for the right people

This theory was created by Paul Hersey and Ken Blanchard and it says that a successful leader is the one who knows how to change the leadership styles based on the maturity of the people he is leading and also based on tasks.

Depending on what's needed to get the job done efficiently, the leader should be more focused on tasks, or more on developing people and making them understand the necessity of their work.

Leadership Styles

There are four leadership styles according to this theory:

a) *Telling (S1)*-Leaders tell their team members what to do and how to do it.
b) *Selling (S2)* - Leaders provide information and direction, but there is more communication with followers. Leaders sell their message to convince people to do tasks.
c) *Participating (S3)* - Leaders focus more on the relationships and less on direction. Leaders work with their team members and share decision-making responsibilities.
d) *Delegating (S4)* - Leaders handle their tasks and responsibilities to their group or team members, but they monitor the progress, being less involved in decisions.

There are two different approaches: S1 and S3 are more focused on getting the job done successfully whereas S2 and S4 are based on developing team members' abilities for working independently.

There are also four distinct levels of maturity of the person or the group you're leading:

a)   M1 - People who are at the bottom level of the scale. They are new in the organization and they lack the knowledge, skills, and confidence in doing their work on their own. This kind of people have to be pushed to take on the task.

b)   M2 - The level where people want to take responsibilities but they still don't have the skills to complete it.

c)   M3 - People who are willing and prepared to help in finishing jobs. They are more skilled than M3, but they are not fully confident in their abilities.

d)   M4 - People who can work individually and are fully confident in their strong skills, being very committed to the task.

This model combines the different leadership styles with the level of maturity that corresponds to each need.

Maturity Level	Most appropriate leadership style
M1: Low maturity	S1: Telling/directing
M2: Medium maturity, limited skills	S2: Selling/coaching
M3: Medium maturity, higher skills but lacking confidence	S3: Participating/supporting
M4: High maturity	S4: Delegating

This model will help you to determine and adopt the appropriate leadership style for each person.

A great leader masters all of them and knows when and how to apply them, achieving performance and developing people to their fullest potential.

Chapter 6: Path-Goal Theory

Discovering the best leadership style

The Path-Goal Theory was developed by Robert House to explain workplace leadership.

It was built on two theories of work motivation.

The first one is goal-setting theory, which highlights that setting challenging but realistic goals and rewarding the team members for achieving the company's goals is the most effective way of motivating them.

The second theory, expectancy theory, explains why people work hard to complete work goals.

There are two beliefs that drive their motivation of achieving work goals:

a. Achieving work goals leads to increase in pay/promotion/status.

b. Their behavior towards the work goal has a huge impact (expectancy) in leading to their personal goal.

This theory is built on the concept that effective leaders are those who inspire and motivate their team to achieve goals.

Leaders are responsible for providing information and necessary support for subordinates by encouraging them to achieve work goals.

The way to do it is to make the effort reward relationship outstanding by linking preferable outcomes to goal realization.

Using this tool, you can identify the best leadership approach, based on people's needs, the tasks they are doing, and the environment they are working in.

It helps you put the right person to work on the fitted task. Think about high-capable people who are assigned to a complex task. They clearly need another leadership approach than people who are not so skilled, who are assigned to ambiguous tasks.

Leadership Responsibilities

If you want to achieve goals and finish the tasks successfully, you have to motivate and support your team.

There are three ways of achieving this:

a. *Helping them identify and achieve their goals.*
b. *Erasing obstacles and improving the performance of the team members*
c. *Rewarding them along the way for finishing their tasks*

There are four leadership styles you should use to motivate and help your team members increase their potential and performance.

#1. *Supportive Leadership* - Leaders from this category tend to focus more on the relationships and the establishment of strong and productive bonds. They show sensitivity to individual team members' needs. The main interest is their team, not the goals of the organization and the way of perceiving them. Performance comes as a great effect of people's work and dedication. When they are motivated, they become engaged in the process. This leadership style is the best when tasks are repetitive or stressful.

2. *Directive Leadership* - Leaders communicate their goals and expectations and also sets clear tasks. This leadership style is best when the goals are unstructured or the tasks are very complicated and the team members are inexperienced for accomplishing them successfully.

3. *Participative Leadership* - This leadership style is based on mutual participation or feedback. Before taking decisions, leaders consult their team and consider their ideas or goals. This leadership style is best when the team has only experienced people, when the task is complex and challenging, and the team members are willing to come out with their input in getting great results.

4. *Achievement-Oriented Leadership* - It is based on giving demanding tasks to the team and the leader is confident in the team's abilities and experience. The leader expects the team to perform very well and he maintains high-standards for everyone. This leadership style is best when the team is unchallenged and unmotivated to finish tasks.

The choice of which leadership style to use depends on two sets of contingency variables.

The first one involves environmental factors that are outside the control of the subordinates such as task structure, authority system, and work group.

The second one concerns individual factors such as personality, experience, abilities, competencies, and motivation.

The path-goal theory highlights the conviction with which effective leaders point out the paths for their subordinates.

Path-Goal theory is a contingency theory based on specifying a leader's style or behavior that best fits the employee and work environment to achieve a goal.

Chapter 7: Six Emotional Leadership Styles

Choosing the right style for the right situation

This tool, developed and explained by Daniel Goleman, Richard Boyantzis, and Annie McKee, describes the six distinct emotional leadership styles, each one with a distinct effect on people's emotions, each one with its strengths and weaknesses in different situations.

Four of them are based on harmony and positive outcomes in the organization: Visionary, Coaching, Affiliative, and Democratic. The others, Commanding and Pace-Setting, can create tension and should be used only in specific situations.

1. The Visionary Leader

Visionary leaders move people towards a shared vision.

They inspire people to believe in a vision and tell them where they are all going, but not how to get there.

They encourage people and give them the opportunity to discover ways to get to the desired outcome.

They give others knowledge power. The more people use it, the more powerful and competent they become in implementing decisions and finding the right path to reach the final goals.

2. The Coaching Leader

This leadership style is based on the leader's ability to clearly define roles and objectives, seeking input and suggestions in the process of decision-making.

Decisions are still made by leaders but their team has a huge impact on the process, so their opinions truly count.

Communication is a key element in exercising this leadership style.

Coaching leaders are very effective in determining where performance and results need improvement.

They provide a lot of guidance, helping others advance their skills and build bench strengths.

They not only develop others, but also provide the direction, encouraging and inspiring people along the way. In this way, they motivate others and make people believe in their expertise power.

3. The Affiliative Leader

Affiliative leaders are masters in establishing positive connections and harmony within the organizations.

This leadership style is built on positive feedback and collaboration.

Emotional needs are more important than work needs.

The main disadvantage is that poor performance is tolerated out of loyalty.

4. Democratic Leader

The democratic leader focuses on decision making by winning consensus, and intense commitment to goals, strategies, and tactics.

They are very flexible in adapting to more effective methods of solving problems and dealing with difficulties.

It encourages the work in teams, where ideas are discussed openly and people are stimulated to come up with new ideas.

This leadership style is efficient in dynamic and rapidly changing environments, where decisions need to be made quickly and effectively. Unfortunately, they might not always be very quick in making the best decisions.

If a decision is very difficult and broad, it is important to have the different areas of expertise represented and contributing input – this is where a democratic leader shines.

5. Commanding Leader

It is the oldest leadership style, also named "military" leadership, but often the least effective.

Commanding leaders are very competitive, driven, assertive, and goal-oriented.

They are very motivated to reach their objectives.

The main objective of this leadership style is immediate compliance. They tell people what to do with no compliance and without listening to people's needs and perspectives.

Because it rarely involves praise and frequently employs criticism, it undercuts morale and job satisfaction.

It is only effective in a crisis, when an urgent turnaround is needed.

Even the modern military has come to recognize its limited usefulness.

6. Pace-Setting Leader

The pace-setting leaders set high standards of performance.

They build challenging and exciting goals for their people, expecting excellence and exemplifying it themselves.

They identify poor performance and help them to develop their skills and succeed.

When it is necessary, they roll up their sleeves and rescue the situation.

But they tend to be bad in guiding people along the way. They believe that people can find the right direction by themselves. This is not so bad, because they give people the freedom to reinvent and find new ways of reaching the desired outcomes. But it is effective only when democratic leaders work only with high-performing and competent teams.

Done badly, it lacks Emotional Intelligence, especially self-management. It can also lead to exhaustion and decline in the long-term because people will be struggling to be effective until they drain all their resources.

One of the most representative phrases that can describe their attitude are: *"If you can't keep up, you shouldn't be on my team,"* or *"If you can't do it right, I'll do it myself."*

They are focused on getting high quality results fast, enforcing superior standards of execution and quickly taking the responsibility away from those who underperform.

This style is often used when employees are highly motivated and do not require manager feedback for further growth.

It often works in fast paced and competitive environments where the direction and objectives are clearly defined.

It can also be used with underperforming employees who are not showing the signs of improvement. In this way, they will be forced to develop their skills and reach the level of knowledge of high performers.

Chapter 8: Transformational Leadership

Becoming an inspirational leader

What is Transformational Leadership?

The concept of transformational leadership was created and developed in 1978 by the leadership expert, James McGregor Burnes.

It is a process where "leaders and followers raise one another to higher levels of morality and motivation."

It is believed to be the most important leadership style in business leadership because it:

1. Represents the integrity and fairness

2. Sets clear goals

3. Establishes high expectations

4. Encourages the team

5. Provides support and reward

6. Makes people look beyond their self-interest

7. Inspires people reach for the improbable

8. Arouses people's emotions

How to Become a Transformational Leader

1. Create an inspiring vision

Crafting an inspiring vision to drive change

What is a vision?

Leaders need to express it, teams and employees want to hear it, but very few people can tell you exactly how to develop one. A vision is created from the hopes, dreams, and aspirations of those you are attempting to lead. If they can't find themselves in the vision, the big picture, how can the leader expect them to understand what they have to do?

When a vision belongs only to the leader, the team can't understand the expectations.

When a vision is shared, taking in account the dreams of the team, it is easy to attract people, maintain a motivated workforce, and give people the strength and confidence to repel hurdles and challenges on the road to building a successful organization.

People will always need a compelling reason to follow a leader, and this is why you should develop and communicate an inspiring vision of the future.

Your vision makes your team or organization's purpose stand out.

Understanding people's values and competencies, the scarceness of the resources they have to use, and conducting a smart analysis of the environment, you can develop your own leadership style.

Use symbolic language. Inspiring leaders use them in their motivational speeches.

They use metaphors and analogies, give examples, tell stories, and relate anecdotes.

Metaphors trigger the right hemisphere of the brain, a critical component for persuasion to occur.

Create word pictures. Use words and images in a presentation and communication that evokes sights, sounds, tastes, smells, and tactile feelings because "People aren't persuaded by the facts as much as are by the emotions, feelings, and images behind those facts."

Practice positive communication. The key for creating a vision is to breed optimism, promote resilience, and renew faith and confidence in the team.

"People actually remember downbeat comments far more often, in greater detail, and with more intensity than they do encouraging words."

This is why a leader should always see the bright side and be positive in his remarks.

Negative remarks can influence the employee, reducing his mental efficiency.

Develop a coherent strategy. The strategy determines the direction and scope of an organization over the long-term.

Michael Porter, one of the greatest strategy experts, said that the strategy defines and communicates an organization's unique position.

It also determines the resources of the organization, and the skills and the competences needed by employees to create the competitive advantage.

Strategies help leaders see the future of the organization and ensure that the day-to-day activities help move the organization in the right direction.

If you want to develop a vision for your team, start with the company's visions and mission and explore the ways in which your team can contribute directly to it.

2. *Motivate people to buy into and deliver the vision*

Start the process by creating your vision and mission statements. They are the words effective leaders use to highlight the direction and the purpose of the company.

They are used to motivate the team and inspire the vision of the future.

Mission statements set out the purpose of the organization and the primary objectives.

They are very powerful drivers of the company's mission.

Vision statements also identify the company's purpose, but they tend to focus on goals and aspirations.

They have the role to inspire and uplift. If the strategy of the company changes, they remain the same during the process.

After setting the mission and vision statement, you have to create a call to action using a business storytelling that will communicate and connect your audience, your team, with the message of your vision.

It will make employees understand the objectives, goals, and desired outcome, and inspire them to work with you for accomplishing those goals.

The vision you have set has to reflect the need of the company and the needs of the employees.

If the only person you are trying to help is yourself, you won't inspire anyone.

You need to link the people's goals and tasks with the company's purpose for determining them to contribute and bring input into the company.

You should also learn motivation techniques.

They will ensure you that people follow your strategy and understand your vision. And most importantly, they are engaged in the process.

3. Manage delivery of the vision

A vision is not valuable until it is not turned into reality.

Many leaders make the mistake of developing a vision, but not putting it into action/delivering it.

For delivering your vision, you should make the necessary changes with the full support of your team.

Clearly communicate the responsibilities of each person and the roles and make the connection with your plan/goal.

Everyone should understand his role within the organization and the importance he has in the process of achieving success and performance.

The next step is to set SMART goals (*Specific, Measurable, Attainable, Relevant, Time-based*).

These are meaningful and challenging goals and objectives that will ensure clarity, commitment, feedback, and task complexity.

One of the books from my portfolio describes the entire process of setting SMART goals in your personal and professional life, based on a complex time management approach.

http://www.amazon.com/Time-Management-Techniques-Developing-Procrastination-ebook/dp/B00TWMAZDO/ref=sr_1_1?s=digital-text&ie=UTF8&qid=1448208926&sr=1-1&keywords=serena+richards

Another aspect of delivering your vision is to stay visible, practicing management by walking around, staying in touch with your team.

This technique is ideal for transformational leadership because it helps you stay connected with daily activities and allows you to respond promptly to challenges and problems as they arise.

Communication is an essential ingredient of successful transformational leadership. Make sure that your message and vision are heard and understood and give clear, regular feedback, so that your people know what you want.

4. Build ever-stronger, trust-based relationships with your people

As a transformational leader, people are the most important asset of the company, the pawns on the chessboard named organization.

You need to focus your attention on their needs and expectations and work hard to help them reach their goals and dreams.

Leadership is a long-term process, and as a leader, you need to work constantly to build relationships, earn trust, and help your people grow as individuals.

Meet your people individually to understand their development needs, and help them to meet their career goals.

What do they want to achieve in their role?

Where do they see themselves five years from now?

How can you help them reach the goal?

You can build trust with your people by being open and honest in your interactions.

Lastly, set aside time to coach your people.

When you help them find their own solutions, you not only create a skilled team, but you also strengthen their self-confidence and their trust in you.

The conception behind transformational leadership is providing and working toward a vision, but also has elements of empowerment, of taking care of people, and even of task orientation.

The job of the transformational leader is not simply to provide inspiration and then disappear. This duty is to be there, day after day, convincing people that the vision is reachable, renewing their commitment, and priming their enthusiasm.

Transformational leaders work harder than anyone else, and in other words "keep their eyes on the prize".

Chapter 9: Developing Expert Power

There are so many different power bases that leaders can use and exploit.

It may include also the problematic power basis such as the power of position, the power to give rewards, the power to punish people, and the power to control information.

Though they manifest some strength, they put the person being lead in an unhealthy position of weakness, while the leader will become autocratic or out of touch.

If we analyze the society we live in, we will notice that it has changed drastically over the last 50 years. People change jobs easier than they did before because they have a lot of job opportunities and society today is mostly based on performance (employees are evaluated and hired based on how skilled they are, not on the need of the organization to fulfill the empty workplace as they did in the past).

And this type of employee can't be manipulated by their leaders as they were in the past.

They have a sort of independence and protection against destructive forms of power. People don't enjoy having power exerted over them, so they will do what they can to undermine leaders who use these sorts of power.

Why? Because they have the right to choose the leader who's going to guide and show the straight directions for reaching outstanding performance.

They want leaders who are able to understand a situation, find or at least suggest solutions, use a solid judgment in taking decisions instead of adopting a subjective approach, employee through knowledge and experience.

People want leaders who demonstrate expertise, so that they can trust leaders' decisions and the moves they make with the aim of achieving high results.

The leader's words have more value when he exerts expert power.

Confidence, decisiveness, and reputation for rational thinking are the main traits of expert leaders.

How to use the tool:

For leaders, this tool is essential because his team looks for someone to guide and enlighten the direction.

They have to believe in a leader's ability to set worthwhile direction, provide sound guidance, and coordinate the achievement of great results.

If the team perceives the leader as an authentic expert, they will listen to him when he is trying to persuade them or inspire them.

If your team members respect your expertise, then they know you want to guide them in working effectively.

If they trust your judgment, then they will trust you when you try to direct their efforts and hard work in such a way that will make the most of their hard work.

If they can see the expertise, then they will truly believe in your competence of directing all their efforts in achieving enormous goals.

Expert power is a key element for motivating team members to perform at their best.

How can you build the expert power?

Expert power is created by building expertise, and this is made by:

1. Promoting an image of expertise

So many work fields perceive expertise as knowledge, experience, and education, so leaders should make their teams, peers, or subordinates aware of their formal education, relevant work experience, and significant achievements.

A relevant tactic to make this information visible is to display your diplomas, awards, licenses, and other evidence of expertise in places where people can see them, such as your office, or you can make subtle references of your past performance and experience.

2. Maintaining credibility

Once the image of expertise is established, the leader should care about maintaining it. He should avoid making careless comments about subjects in which he is very poorly informed or being associated in unsuccessful projects.

3. Act confidently and decisively in a crisis

In moments of crisis, employees need a leader who comes up with effective solutions and takes charge of the impact they have. They need someone to show them how to cope with problems. In that moment, they begin perceiving the knowledge and the promptness of leaders with expert power.

Leaders should never express doubts or appear confused in front of their team because they risk losing their influence.

4. Keep informed

One of the most efficacious way of obtaining expert power is to stay well-informed of the development of the team, the company's performance, and the efficiency of your leadership style. Leaders should demonstrate their expertise and the ability to persuade through knowledge. Knowledge is power.

5. Recognize subordinate concerns

Great leaders listen carefully to the needs, concerns and the uncertainties of their team members.

6. Avoid threatening the self-esteem of subordinates

Expert power is based on the knowledge differential between team members and leaders. This incongruity can damage the relationship between leader and his team if he doesn't exercise his expert power wisely.

If the leader acts in a superior way, team members may dislike the status comparisons between them and their leader and they may discredit him.

Also, some leaders present their ideas with an air of patronizing superiority that might influence people's perspective about their position; they will feel like the leader treats them as if they are ignorant.

Power comes from everywhere and in different forms, so a leader's mission is to handle each type.

The psychologist, Nicole Lipkin, affirmed that *"Power tends to get to people's heads"/"We're not really trained to handle power well."*

Expert power is an immense source of superior knowledge. It is based on continual learning and improvement. But it also requires skills, talent, and ethical behavior.

Management By Objectives (MBO)

How to Align Objectives with Organizational Goals

If you were wondering how you can align employees' objectives with the organization goals, management by objectives is the most useful approach.

Using management by objectives in the leadership practice is a very helpful tool for motivation and engagement of people in the process of achieving organization's mission.

The developer of the concept was Peter Druker, one of the fathers of management and promoted it in the popular book, *The Practice of Management*, with the aim of bringing people and managers' needs in the same line, by making people understand their contribution in the process of reaching goals and also determining managers/ leaders consider peoples' needs and help them develop themselves through work experience.

The essence of MBO is the participative goal setting, choosing a course of action, and decision making.

It helps leaders establish the standards for performance, measure the employees' actual performance, and compare it with the standards set with the aim of improving their yield.

Peter Drucker's perspective was that people involved in goal setting and choosing the course of action will be more receptive and they will understand their responsibilities more clearly.

The system was described as a process where the manager and the employee find common goals, define the individual major areas of responsibility in terms of the outcomes expected by them, and measure the progress and the implication of others in the process.

MBO helps employees have a clear understanding of their roles and the duties expected of them, so they can understand how their activities contribute to the accomplishment of companies' goals.

This approach is based on fulfilling the personal goals of each employee.

And it does this with the following benefits:

1. Motivation

Leaders should empower people to make decisions and assume their acts. When this happens, employees are more committed and they feel some kind of job satisfaction that motivates them to work effectively.

2. Better communication and coordination

Better communication leads to harmonious relationships within the organization. In an environment where people get along very well, the constant review is promoted and sustained, while people enjoy receiving objective feedback of their performance so they can understand what they are doing wrong and fix/improve it.

3. Goals' clarity

4. Subordinates tend to have a higher commitment to objectives they set for themselves than those imposed on them by another person.

5. Managers can ensure that the subordinates' objectives are linked to the organization's objectives.

6. Common goal for whole organization means it is a unifying, directive principle of management.

The Mechanism

The MBO process is divided into six steps. All of them are important because they compose a system that works only if all subsystems work effectively.

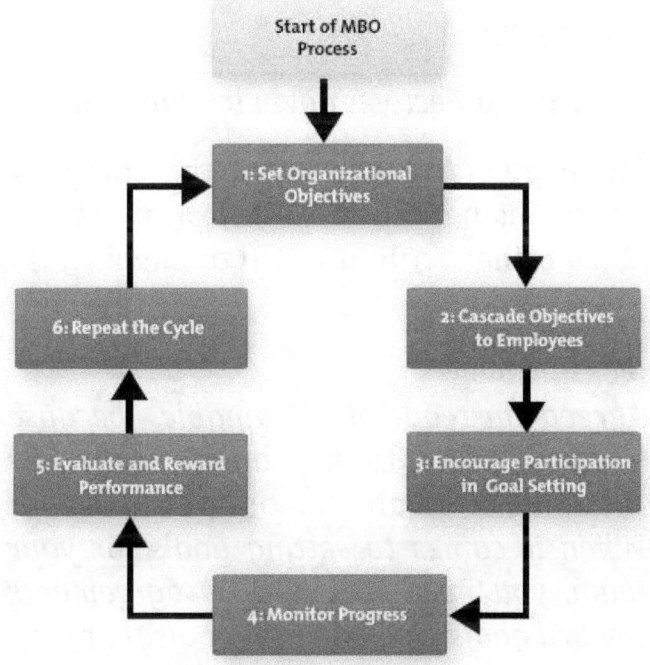

1. Set organizational objectives

Firstly, managers set the main objectives of the organization. They determine the mission and the strategic goals. The objectives they set have to be clear and challenging.

2. Cascade objectives down to employees

The strategic objectives of the company are set using the S.M.A.R.T. framework, which brings structure and trackability:

- *Specific*
- *Measurable*
- *Agreed instead of Attainable, because "agreed" relates to the team context, while "attainable" relates to the personal one. When it comes to setting goals for your team, you need to get their agreements toward goals. You can't set goals that your team is not able to accomplish.*
- *Realistic*
- *Time-based*

These goals are cascaded down from level to level because they need to be understood and approved by employees. It is not enough to set the goals at the top level of management. You need to make people understand the purpose of the goals and how these goals' achievement contributes to their performance and the company's mission.

3. Encourage participation in goal setting

Everyone needs to understand how personal goals fit within the objectives of the company and allow sharing and discussion so that everyone understands "why" things are being done.

Self-direction, decision making, and responsibility are fundamental parts of this step and encourage motivation within the employees.

4. Monitor progress

Because you have used the SMART framework for setting measurable goals and objectives, now you can monitor them.

You need to make sure if they are timely with their monitoring, in case something goes wrong and you have to make adjustments or corrections.

The best way to monitor goal performance and accountability is to divide the goal into smaller goals.

5. Evaluate and reward performance

The MBO process is designed to enhance performance in all levels of the organization.

Employees are evaluated on their performance related to the goals.

They are rewarded and compensated for their efforts and they receive appropriate feedback and also provide it.

6. Repeat the cycle

After the process is completed, the cycle is usually repeated after a review of the previous five-stage process is done and those who were involved in the attainable goals understand the importance of measurable goals and clear performance within the MBO.

Management by Objectives is a powerful tool for aligning employees' actions with an organization's goals.

Chapter 10: Key Performance Indicators (KPIs)

How to Align the Day-to-Day Activities with the Vision and Strategy

There is a continuous pressure to achieve performance targets and increase its levels within the organization.

Managers are mostly focused on ensuring that people support the goals of the organization and work toward accomplishing them.

Performance management is the notion that illustrates the way performance is managed within the organization.

Managers who are focused on people's performance constantly try to answer to the following question:

"How well is an employee applying his or her current skills, and to what extent is he or she achieving the outcomes desired?"

To answer to this question, managers analyze the reports of the performance evaluation for each employee and discover how well an employee has performed his responsibilities.

Key Performance Indicators came to solve the problem of performance on the organizational and individual levels.

In businesses, on the organizational level,

KPI is a measurable value that demonstrates how effectively an organization is reaching key business objectives.

Many organizations use the key performance indicators to measure the success of achieving targets.

Fundamental Leadership KPIs

1. Develop the decision-making ability of leaders

Effective decision-making is the result of combining leadership development efforts with organization culture. If leaders are not so good at decision-making, then they should determine the factors that trigger them.

2. Focus on creativity to unleash peoples' effectiveness

Creativity is one of the core leadership competencies that brings forth high performance and encourages leaders to learn from the past mistakes, and keeps them from repeating the past.

Creativity makes people think outside the box, stretching and fighting to find the best solutions.

Creative teams derive from leaders' ability to instill freedom of expression and encouragement of people to come up with innovative ideas.

3. Increase leadership emphasis on cultural alignment

The pressure that exists in prioritizing the smart working is increasing as the change constantly appears, so leaders have to focus on what needs to be done quickly/on time.

Prioritization is very important for increasing performance. It shows how to align the tasks, projects, and priorities with the stated cultural values and commitments of the organization.

4. Increase leadership communication

If you want to kill a team, block the communication channels within it. There's nothing more destructive for a team than a lack of communication. If people involved in the process don't communicate, then chaos is irreversible. Messages have to be clean and constant to respect the vision.

5. Focus on improving employee performance via managers

The main problem with performance management is that there is a constant struggle for correct implementation.

Performance can be achieved through coaching.

Coaching is the most powerful tool for skills-building and knowledge transfer within the organization, magnifying development on both personal and professional areas.

Change is a key motivator of coaching.

Coaching people through change is the most powerful expertise a leader can exercise.

It is tremendously important that people perceive change as an opportunity to unleash their potential, build new habits, strengthen old competencies, and cultivate new skills.

People tend to perceive change as an intruder, something that unveils their weaknesses and shortcomings in front of managers or colleagues.

As the human nature dictates our behavior and impulses, people don't like to show their weaknesses because they feel more vulnerable in front of others. They fear that others will try to destroy their personality raw

Chapter 11: Motivating People to Deliver the Vision

"Where there is no vision, people perish"

True leaders recognize that they can't do and know everything by themselves.

They value the potential of the people they work amongst.

Their purpose is to motivate, develop, and inspire people.

Leadership is about helping people to perform at their best.

Leaders should inspire and put premium grade rocket fuel into their team.

That fuel is a potent mixture of motivation, ability, and focus.

How is motivation created? There are people who possess a tremendous source of intrinsic motivation, but leaders should create an external motivation pull.

They recognize that people tend to move towards a vision of the future. Leaders create the vision and they communicate it clearly to their people. People follow a direction inspired by the leaders' vision.

People identify their goals in the vision and try to accomplish them indirectly, by becoming engaged in transforming the vision in reality.

This means that people don't need to be pushed to work toward a goal because they have their own impetus.

Successful leaders seem to naturally create harmonious, happy environments, where people love to work together to accomplish the company's goals because they know that this will enhance their productivity and performance, shaping their values and characters.

Leaders naturally create habits where people work as teams, not individually, to accomplish the mission.

How should leaders motivate their people?

They can do this by using sound motivational principles and developing people's competencies.

Today's pace of change makes leaders more careful about the way they motivate people or teams, because they have to implement strategic, fast, and well-crafted decisions and this leads to less time left for making people understand their roles.

If leaders don't inspire people to believe in the potential of a goal, they will become confused and demotivated.

When leaders develop their people, they also protect the future of their organization. People and organizations are intrinsically linked.

People who are focused on a vision and understand what they are doing, know how to do it, and most importantly, why they are doing it.

Motivated people deliver their value to the accomplishing of organization's goals.

Motivation stands in the ability to understand what drives people, to communicate, to involve, to challenge, to encourage, to set up an example, to develop and coach, to give and receive feedback, and then reward people for their efforts.

"Motivation is about cultivating your human capital. The challenge lies not in the work itself, but in you, the person who creates and manages the work environment."

Others Books By Serena Richards

Now, if you were delighted by the content of this book and the value I have put in it, I invite you to read my books from the same category.

The *Leadership Coaching* book is a delightful coalescence of coaching with leadership expertise.

http://www.amazon.com/Leadership-Coaching-Performance-Potential-Techniques-ebook/dp/B00UENDJ92/ref=sr_1_4?s=digital-text&ie=UTF8&qid=1449699333&sr=1-4&keywords=serena+richards

The *Team Leadership* book covers the main principles of leadership and management. Their alluring fusion gives birth to a unique leadership style based on leadership traits and management exercise.

It seems that a great manager can't completely fulfill the needs of his followers without mastering the leadership knowledge and ability to transcend the visible limits of people's character.

http://www.amazon.com/Team-Leadership-Manage-Highly-Effective-ebook/dp/B018T5PF84/ref=sr_1_1?s=digital-text&ie=UTF8&qid=1449699333&

sr=1-
1&keywords=serena+richards

The *Passive income* book covers the need of financial freedom and provides multiple effective ways to change the main aspect that drains the humanity- the lack of money.

http://www.amazon.com/Passive-Income-Effective-Successful-Financial-ebook/dp/B00V5INXPA/ref=sr_1_6?s=digital-text&ie=UTF8&qid=1449699333&sr=1-6&keywords=serena+richards

In case you love to risk and gain money from investing in different sources of income generation such

as bonds and stocks, my book –
"Wall Street Insights" might help you
reach a well-grounded
understanding of the Investing
System.

http://www.amazon.com/Wall-
Street-Insights-Well-Grounded-
Understanding-
ebook/dp/B013GQ0ST2/ref=sr_1_5
?s=digital-
text&ie=UTF8&qid=1449699333&sr
=1-5&keywords=serena+richards

Conclusion

Your leadership style defines the organization.

It not only increases its performance, but also encourages the development of teams and followers.

It is based on exercising power, gaining the privileges of high status, task orientation, empowerment, and the ability of being the right boss, when is necessary.

A great leader knows that the secret of successful leadership stands in the ability to master all the leadership styles and adapt each style to the suitable situation.